Reiki For Beginners

The Ultimate Reiki Guide That Teaches You All You Need To Know About Reiki Healing & Improving Your Life With The Power Of Reiki!

Table Of Contents

Introduction — v

Chapter 1: Understanding Reiki Beyond the Spiritual Field — 1

Chapter 2: Grasping the Roots of Reiki, How It Can Influence your Practice, and How to Apply it in Your Practice — 7

Chapter 3: Triggering Healing Energy Through Personal Spiritual Pursuit and Through a Reiki Master — 17

Chapter 4: A Quick Guide on Hand Placements for Specific Ailments — 27

Conclusion — 33

Introduction

I want to thank you and congratulate you for downloading the book, *"Reiki For Beginners"*.

This book contains helpful information about Reiki, what it is, and how to use it.

You will soon discover the history of Reiki, the theories behind it, and some scientific proof of its power!

Reiki is a form of energy healing that has been slowly growing in popularity. Stories of its powers and benefits are spreading, and more and more people are seeking this form of treatment.

This book includes tips and techniques to help beginners master the art of Reiki healing in no time! This includes healing yourself, and also strategies for healing other people.

You will learn how to unblock your energy flow, and different hand positions you can use for self-healing with Reiki!

This book will serve as a great guide for beginners, and get you started with Reiki healing from the comfort of your home!

Thanks again for downloading this book, I hope you enjoy it!

Chapter 1: Understanding Reiki Beyond the Spiritual Field

Reiki Healing

Unlike common therapies where healers perform processes that, in some ways, alter the physical conditions of the body as with acupuncture and massage, or where healers require patients to ingest, apply or inhale herbs and its by-products, reiki heals using only the light touch of hands. In other words, it is internally and externally non-manipulative in the physical aspect. What it does, however, is restore balance to your body by harmonizing your "life force energy", or as the Chinese call it, "Chi" or "Qi".

Do not mistake this, however, for a religion. Because of the presence of the word "spiritual" in the healing process, many Westerners baselessly conclude that one needs to believe in a specific set of ethereal beings and beliefs to receive reiki treatments. Reiki has got to do with biomagnetism, and every person on the planet emits this. Therefore, it does not discriminate based on religion.

Effects of Reiki

As nonsensical as it may sound, the foundations of reiki are that by restoring balance to the spiritual aspect of the body, the healing of everything else will follow.

Reiki can heal the simplest of symptoms like fatigue and physical pain, to complex illnesses like cancer -- although the latter is yet to be continuously observed in humans. However, it is more commonly used in the US as a stress reduction and relaxation therapy. Other times, when the patient is undergoing a series of surgeries or is recovering from broken and fractured bones, they complement it with reiki therapy to help them cope with unbearable, agonizing pain.

What separates reiki from other therapies is how it boosts the body's immune system. Therefore, not only will the person recover from whatever ailment they have, they will maintain an overall healthy well-being and resist future bodily threats.

Who Performs Reiki?

Reiki can actually be learned and practiced by anyone, it's not just for monks who live in mountaintops as you may be imagining right now. As long as you have every intent to heal another person, and even yourself, you can perform this mind-boggling therapy. Age isn't a defining factor either. Even children can give reiki treatments as long as they have the know-how. At the same time, anyone can also receive reiki, even animals.

Reiki and Modern Science

It is no secret that many are sceptical about this miracle, especially those from the medical field. Because of the fact that the body's life force, or chi, is invisible and immeasurable, the general public have come to suppose that Reiki is fictitious.

Reiki Vs. Placebo

Despite the many positive testimonies of the treatment, sceptics blame the results on placebo. According to them, the reason why patients heal from reiki therapy is because they *believe* it works, thus creating the placebo effect. This is a scientifically proven fact -- the body does make physical changes according to the beliefs established by the mind. Study results, however, have proved reiki's validity, and at the same time, debunked the above said theory.

Krinsley D. Bengston, an average reiki sceptic, witnessed several cases of cancer remission under the miraculous hands of a hands-on energy healer. To prove if the therapy really relied on a placebo effect, he himself learned reiki and reproduced the healing effects on mice afflicted with breast cancer. According to records, the poor creatures would inevitably die 14 to 27 days following injection. After dedicating an hour to reiki treatment every day for thirty days, however, the cancer disappeared completely, and the mice lived happily for their normal lifespans. Another group of mice injected with the same illness, on the other hand, were not given any reiki treatment and all died within the abovementioned time frame.

The same experiment was done by other volunteers -- all sceptics -- and 87.9% of the reiki treated mice were cured from cancer, while the other cancer-induced group, again, all died. What's amazing from this study was how the reiki-treated group's immunity against the same illness greatly improved. After surviving the cancer, they were once again injected with the same thing by researchers. Surprisingly, however, the mice resisted the illness and remained cancer-free.

With this, Bengston finally concluded that one does not need full belief of reiki to practice and reproduce its healing effects, that the process and its results are plausible, and that the effects will improve immunity against the same illness.

The Science

Another thing skeptics fail to understand is that the world has forces invisible to the naked eye. According to Einstein's theory, mass and energy come hand in hand. To normal human beings, mass is the only visible property between the two, whereas energy will only be felt or seen when an object is moved, for example. Therefore, many are under the understanding that there is no energy in any stationary mass. In reality, however, everything that has mass has energy, and so do us humans.

Comic books, anime, and video games portray this very well. Picture those characters with flaming light around their body as they simply stand (or hover). Although theirs is exaggerated, you are shrouded by the same mysterious power, and in scientific terms, this is called the biomagnetic field.

This is where Andre-Marie Ampere comes in. According to the father of electrodynamics, as long as there are conductors, electrical currents will flow through. Metals and wires are the most commonly known conductors, and despite receiving no electrical shock from holding one, it does not mean they don't have currents. Very low frequencies exist, and though you can't feel them, this remains a form of energy.

Now according to Ampere's law, whatever conducts electricity creates a magnetic field. And you may or may not know this already, but living tissue also is a good conductor of electricity -- the very reason why you get shocked when high currents or voltages flow through you. This means that every cell in your body, including the brain, heart, liver, and all your other organs, are conductors. And by following the laws of physics, it can be safely concluded that you are a living magnetic field, hence the term biomagnetic field.

Science, Medicine and Spirituality

Interestingly, there is a science called magnetobiology -- and this is not about Magneto's physiology. This branch of biophysics studies and observes how magnetic fields affect living systems. Its results then gave way to advancements in the medical field. Various energy-based technologies that can diagnose and treat patients emerged and helped doctors save lives, such as MRI (magnetic resonance imaging), defibrillators, lasers, and more. With this, it can be concluded that the utilization of biomagnetic fields in the medical field has been ongoing for quite some time.

As further studies are made, researchers have found that pulsing magnetic fields serve as defibrillators to tissues, bones and the rest of your body. It means that it has the capacity to trigger healing.

Now, how do all these scientific tales connect to reiki? You probably have an idea already, and if it involves frequencies and hands, then you guessed correctly.

A doctor named John Zimmerman observed and measured the frequencies produced by reiki practitioners' biomagnetic fields. He later discovered that these healers' hands emit around 0.3 to 30 cycles per second, the hertz within the ELF (extremely low frequencies) range. Whether it's by accident or not, these numbers are associated with healthy organs and tissue, and they transmit the exact measure needed to heal the recipient. For example, if the patient is suffering from ligament damage, their body will then require 10 Hz to jumpstart the healing. As for bone growth, 7 Hz is needed. While in nerve regeneration, a low 2 Hz is enough. And for capillary formation, a high 15 Hz will do the trick. What's even more amazing about this discovery is how they can influence the electric currents of those in close proximity, hence the light touch of healers on recipients.

The awesomeness doesn't stop there. As explained earlier, everything that has mass has energy, and one form of it is electric currents. If you have a biomagnetic field which can be measured in frequencies, then so does the earth -- this includes the grass you walk on, the trees and plants around you, and all the rest that makes up our home planet. According to scientists, the electromagnetic spectrum of earth is at 7.83 Hz. Many refer to this as the "tuning fork", because once living things entertain this rhythm, it will generate natural healing properties.

Do not mistake the word "entertain", however, by playing a guitar and singing a song to mother earth. This may sound hippie, but it simply means you have to have the same frequency or same vibration as the world. In other words, you have to synchronize with this tuning fork, and amazingly, reiki practitioners are during the process of healing.

All this is from the point of view of scientists, however. Although reiki therapists aren't particularly informed of all this magnetobiology and physics stuff, if you ask them what they do when they heal, they will more or less say they are merely channeling "universal energy" to the patient. But now that you know more about the science behind it, you can safely conclude that what they are saying still rings true, because they do synchronize with the earth and serve as conductors of "universal *frequencies*" which trigger healing in recipients.

Now of course, wounds and broken bones won't heal in a matter of minutes, like in the movies. Reiki is a form of therapy, and like other treatments the patient needs to religiously attend sessions for weeks or months.

Chapter 2: Grasping the Roots of Reiki, How It Can Influence your Practice, and How to Apply it in Your Practice

Now that you have an understanding of the science behind reiki, and realize that it's not just some baseless trending therapy, it's time to grasp the spiritual side of the practice. This healing technique has got to do with how well you connect to your inner self and the universe within you. Yes, you know what frequency is needed to transmit healing hands, but do you know how to achieve that? The first step towards this is knowing the history of how reiki was discovered and understanding the general principles that govern it.

You may feel eager to learn how to perform treatments, but also understand that this is also a discipline, and that means you have to understand every aspect of it before jumping in to performing it. So please, do not skip this section of the book.

The Different System of Beliefs that Gave Birth to Reiki

Surprisingly, reiki hasn't been in existence for thousands of years as you may have imagined. It only actually started around 93 years ago (sometime in the early 1920's) in Japan, and the man behind it was Mikao Usui. He was a monk, and during his time, Shinto, Taoist, and Buddhist lineages coexisted and served as the main themes of culture and spirituality among the Japanese.

Note!

This book will purposely elaborate more on the different system of beliefs to provide a holistic view on how the many variations of Eastern religions work. As mentioned earlier, Western religions are structured and taught very differently. Although there is no need to switch beliefs to simply learn reiki, you are in danger of misunderstanding some of the important aspects of the practice. You need to enter the minds of the masters from the East to fully grasp what disciplines and mindsets they followed to perform treatments. Reiki, after all, is not about following a predetermined set of instructions with steps one to X. It is more than that, and you will discover this by reading onward.

Each of these beliefs, philosophies, and ways of living (whatever you want to call it) has its own unique set of principles, but if you take a step back and look at the bigger picture, you will notice how similar they all are. They all move in the same spiritual precept that is very unlike Western religious beliefs. Many of these are focused on spiritual growth through self-discovery, and that deities and other figures are all based on energy and natural forces, or are real mortal people who have simply attained enlightenment as with Buddha. With all this being said, it is not surprising that all of these factors have minor and major contributions to the founding of Reiki.

Usui was a Tendai Buddhist monk. Buddhism has many different branches, and although they have the same goal of bringing enlightenment to anyone who wishes to follow the discipline, their processes are different. As for Tendai, Shintoism was deemed as its roots. The main symbol of Shinto is the Torii Gate -- those giant red gate-like structures found across the country. This religion or system of beliefs is focused on giving respect to spirits and energies bound in all aspects of nature such as plants, animals, and even the elements. At the same time, Tendai also has roots that can be traced back in China and then to Tibet. According to experts, it shares many sutras with Vajrayana Buddhism, which has its focus on esoteric energy practices, or in simpler terms, chakra work, and this may primarily be where Usui learned to practice with energy. Biographers also account his experiences and training with Shugendo, a kind of Japanese shamanism exclusively practiced within the mountainous areas where Usui lived. This, along with Shinto and Buddhism, laid the foundation of the hands-on healing method in reiki.

Other possible disciplines Usui may have studied prior to the founding of reiki, according to his biographers, are Shingon, Pure Land Buddhism, and many other Japanese Buddhist practices with uncanny relationships with Vajrayana Buddhism. Despite their differences, they share the same lineage to Mahayana Buddhism, where its main belief was how enlightenment can be achieved at any moment, rather than in a long multi-life spiritual process.

Bearing all the knowledge of these different practices, Usui was said to have formed and formalized reiki when he attended a 21-day Buddhist Retreat back in 1922.

The Reiki Mind Frame

Before elaborating on the four (or sometimes three) degrees of reiki, which you need to learn before proceeding with learning to apply hands-on treatments, you need to know the general mind frame that needs to be adopted to perform energy healing. This will greatly affect the effectiveness of your treatments and the flow of energy throughout your body. And later on, another scientific explanation will once again be presented to support these seemingly groundless claims.

The reason why many mistake Reiki for a religion is because of the various precepts one has to learn in order to heal. If you are familiar with the very basic principles of the above enumerated Buddhism branches, you will notice that reiki basically follows the same, only under different titles. Nonetheless, it will all boil down to enlightenment, or at least the road leading to it -- and it is through *loving kindness and compassion.*

This is the very core of reiki, and you cannot perform treatments, or at least, be efficient at it, if you do not exude loving kindness and compassion. All the rest are but guidelines and principles on *how* to achieve this frame of mind. Although many are under the impression that these two are rooted at the heart because they are defined as feelings, Buddhism actually teaches that these are in fact the fruits of our thoughts. The budding of these two will begin at how you perceive the world, accept the truth, and detach yourself from worldly attachments.

The Science of Loving Kindness and Compassion

Going back to the discussion of electric currents and such, another fact about magnetic fields is that they are not uniform in every part of the body. The brain produces its own, the same way the hands independently emit one. Among all of them, the one that generates the strongest and largest magnetic field is the heart. **It can project energy up to fifteen feet, and produces a magnetic field 100 times stronger than the brain's.**

What's more stunning about these findings was when researchers measured the frequencies when two people touch. Based on the results, the electromagnetic energy radiated by the heart is transferred and reciprocated upon contact, and that peaks were measured specifically on the surface where the other person touches.

This is where love and compassion comes in. According to a research director from the Institute of HeartMath, Rollin McCraty, having these feelings generates a specific frequency in the biomagnetic field that affects living tissues in a highly beneficial way. If the intention of love and compassion is sustained, the frequency will become powerful enough to affect and activate changes in water and even DNA structures.

With these amazing results on hand, researchers have concluded that if a healer can establish a deeper sense of loving kindness and caring, the energy he or she produces will be more coherent, and will thus produce greater effects on tissue repair.

Building Loving Kindness and Compassion Through Buddhist Teachings

Despite the many branches and various interpretations of followers and masters, the core of Buddhism is instilled in the Four Noble Truths and the Eightfold Path. Once you familiarize yourself with these principles, you will begin to understand how to eliminate the many negative aspects of life and living. And with these gone, your mind and heart will soon pave way for loving kindness and compassion, and then for enlightenment.

This book is about reiki, so despite deserving a separate chapter, there will only be a brush over on the details of the abovementioned principles. Do not undermine its importance, however. Knowing these will give you a sturdy foundation of loving kindness and compassion, which then has a great effect on your reiki practice.

Note!

You will have to apply these teachings in everyday life to learn how to easily tap into love and caring. Besides, it will do you good not only during times of healing; life will practically become brighter and easier to handle, and it will also attract good karma.

- ❖ **The Four Noble Truths**
    - ➢ 1: The Truth About Suffering
      The first noble truth basically states that to live is to suffer. No person on earth is immune to the imperfections that comes along with life, and these mainly are pain, illness and disease, aging, and death.

    - ➢ 2: The Truth About the Source of Suffering
      According to Buddha, the source of suffering are attachments, may it be to material things, people, or experiences. People rest their happiness on these things, but once it disappears, they experience suffering. This will then cause them to crave for more of these to sustain a happy life, but what they do not understand is how these attachments will only cage them in a never-ending loop of wanting for more.

    - ➢ 3: The Truth About the Cessation of Suffering
      Just like a good doctor, after describing the illness and its causes, Buddha also explains that there is a way to separate yourself from attachments, and thus free yourself from suffering.

    - ➢ 4: The Truth About the Path that Leads to the Cessation of Suffering

The road towards the cessation of suffering has been elaborated in the principles under the Eightfold Path.

❖ The Eightfold Path

Before proceeding, understand that the following are not a series of steps and that you need to follow and apply them one by one. Every path supports the rest, so if you are to embrace one, you have to embrace all.

- ### The Right View
  To see the world as it is and in its true nature -- without labels, tags, discretion, or any kind of judgement -- is the wisdom behind the right view. For example, a woman in skimpy clothes walked past you, and you immediately assumed she's a prostitute. Through the eyes of an individual aiming to share loving kindness and compassion, however, she is but a woman -- nothing else.

- ### The Right Intention
  Although you do not act or show your craving, hatred, bad intentions, and such on something, you still thought of it, and that is as important as doing it, because actions and speech starts in the mind. Just like with love and caring, you will not truly feel this and much less act this, if you have the intention to bring harm on another person. There are three main right intentions under the Buddhist doctrine:
    1. Intention of renunciation
    2. Intention of good will
    3. Intention of harmlessness
- ### The Right Speech

There are four rules under the right speech and these are:

1. Do not deceive or tell lies
2. Do not slander and defame others
3. Avoid speaking rude, impolite and abusive words
4. Refrain from engaging in gossip or idle talk

Because of the illusion created by right of speech, many have come to think that expressing their hatred over something, or distaste over someone in a rude manner is alright. In the Western World, this may not be much of a big deal at all, and such words may even be praised and seen as courage, and it might be so. This, however, will only harbor more hatred and greater distaste, not only to themselves, but to others as well. And to cultivate genuine loving kindness and compassion, you must sincerely aim to maintain harmony and peace.

➢ The Right Action

The precepts under this path are similar to those from most other religions, and of course, ethical social conduct.

1. Do not kill
2. Do not steal
3. Never misuse sex
4. Do not lie
5. Never abuse alcohol and other intoxicants

Of course, the above said are extremes, but what's more important in the right action is to act without selfish attachment to your work, and to move without harbouring discord to your environment and community.

- The Right Livelihood
  Along with the right action and right speech, having the right livelihood still moves within the circle of ethical conduct. As long as the job you enter does not break the precepts outlined under the right action, then you are alright. If, however, the very nature of the company you work for opposes the precepts -- for example, you are a bartender, and you induce discord by serving alcohol, but it's your job -- then as long as you do it with pure honesty, Buddhism will have to make way.

- The Right Effort
  The right effort is the perfect complement of the right view and the right action, because in this path, you are encouraged to cultivate positive qualities and prevent negative ones from arising. There are four simple rules under this path and these are:

    1. The effort to inhibit unwholesome qualities from arising.
    2. The effort to eliminate unwholesome qualities that have already risen.
    3. The effort to develop wholesome qualities.
    4. The effort to sustain and intensify wholesome qualities that have already risen.

- The Right Mindfulness
  In the Buddhist context, when you are mindful, it means you are present in the here and now. You are able to maintain complete awareness with your surroundings and with your own

body. At the same time, you push judgmental thoughts away (which is what you need to do according to the Eightfold Path's Right View), because it takes effort to transfer all the attention of your mind on the little things in yourself and the big things around you.

> ➢ The Right Concentration
> The right concentration is meditation, and different Buddhist sects have different ways of doing this. You may be thinking that you won't need this because you're not entirely after enlightenment, but meditation will bring you peace, and with this will harbor loving kindness and compassion. Furthermore, you get to quiet the storms in your mind, and you learn to listen to the air, and these are important skills needed to perform reiki.

Being *spiritual* isn't about getting VIP access to the energy fridge of gods and other ethereal beings. It's really more about learning how to control the thoughts that enter your mind and the words and actions that will then resonate from it. In other words, cultivating loving kindness and compassion will not magically come to you at the snap of a finger. It's all about conditioning your mind, and this is where effort, discipline and patience come in to play.

With that in mind, reiki is not as simple as merely touching the part of the body that aches. This is not the work of a miracle. Just like everything else in our imperfect world, you will have to work to develop this skill. Unlike modern medicine, however, where healing is learned through years of study, memorization and actual application, cultivating the power to heal in reiki will begin from within. The effectivity of the therapy will come from how well you can control and channel unseen forces, and that's what this chapter aimed to help you with.

Chapter 3: Triggering Healing Energy Through Personal Spiritual Pursuit and Through a Reiki Master

The previous chapter discussed how to sustain reiki energy throughout your body, but how do you get it to flow in the first place? There are two ways to do this, 1) through your own spiritual pursuit and 2) through attunement.

Hands-on Energy Healing through Personal Spiritual Pursuit

Some hands-on energy healers manage to activate their healing chi on their own. There is no actual step-by-step process for this, for each experience is unique. Hence, if your mind and heart are open enough, you will not need the assistance of reiki masters to attain and improve your healing abilities. There are even some individuals who have attained master level without the assistance of senior healers.

However, many experts believe that activating energies on one's own cannot be considered reiki. They explain that humans carry a variety of energies, and that a specific set needs to be activated for the purpose of reiki healing.

Imagine buying medicine. There are branded drugs, and these are the ones that get advertised under a brand name which is a lot easier to remember than the name of the chemical. And of course, there are the unnamed ones called generic drugs. These carry almost the same set of chemicals, and it provides the same relief as with the branded ones, but they just aren't the same. The same goes for reiki and self-activated energy healing. Although you cannot directly address the latter as reiki, you also cannot discredit its ability to heal.

How to Unblock Energy Flows

The first thing you need to know about energies is that they're innate. You have these flowing through your body just like how the earth has rivers flowing through it. There are many possibilities as to why you cannot feel and utilize it, but the most common cause are blockages.

Several factors can lead to energy blocks and these range from physiological imbalances to emotional distresses. Below are some potential causes:

- *When the body is polluted by metals, chemicals and atomic toxins, or when poisoned or intoxicated.* Understand that being polluted does not necessarily mean that the person is dying. If you are an average human being with a liking for processed food, then chemicals are constantly present in your body. And if you cook your meals in aluminium pans and saucers, small metal pieces -- microscopic fragments of the pan -- will mix with your food which you will eventually consume. As for poison and intoxicants, alcohol is actually the number one substance that slowly poisons the body.
- *Unreleased or held back emotions.* It is true that when you keep things to yourself, negative emotions such as anxiety, worry and even despair will begin to brew and these can block energy flows.
- *Negative thoughts imposed on you.* The people around you affect you greatly, and sometimes, you are not aware of it. Negative thoughts are sometimes not caused by your lack of emotional release, but from the

simple comments planted by others, like "your teeth are too big" or "you can't learn that; it's too advanced for you". These can breed insecurities and hesitations, which then blocks energies.
- *Unwelcome memories and experiences.* These are different from held emotions because these are not just mere feelings. Events from the past can haunt a person forever and the emotions attached to these memories are what's blocking energy pathways. An individual will find it more difficult to let go of these because of how deeply rooted they are in the mind and in the heart.

Take note of the above blockage causes, because understanding them may just be the secret to unlocking your universal energy. As previously stated, practicing hands-on energy healing will require spiritual aptitude, and the best way to develop this is through self-reflection, and of course, meditation. In other words, you need to know yourself in and out -- your fears, your likes, the things that make you happy, and the memories you can't let go -- and from there, work on releasing each. Never battle these emotions and thoughts, nor deny them. They are a part of you and you simply need to let them go. Remember the Buddhist teachings outlined in the previous chapter. They can guide you through this process, and eventually, help you unblock your chi.

Apart from this, however, there are other habits and states of mind you must adapt to release your energies. This, after all, is a united effort of the body, mind, and heart, thus you need to keep these three in check and in a healthy state.

1. *Unblocking energies in the body.*
   The blood that flows through your veins is the physical representation of your energies. Although it's not the entirety of your chi, it contributes significantly

to your vibration. Therefore, you need to take care of it, and there's no other way to do that than through proper diet and exercise.

You need to eat the right food. Those that contain too much cholesterol, trans-fats, and oils can create blockages in your arteries. This can later lead to heart attacks, but before it reaches that point, it will create disruptions in the flow of you blood and oxygen throughout your body. This means it will be harder for you to breathe, exert even minor physical efforts, and to simply be happy. The same goes for the other systems of your body. Your muscles and bones carry energies as well, so you need to keep them healthy and strong.

Aside from eating foods rich in essential vitamins and nutrients, your body needs ample exercise to boost the flow of energies in your body, and unlock pathways your chi never knew existed. You can engage in activities you enjoy doing, but if you are really aiming to channel universal energies, then you are recommended to learn and practice tai chi. This rather slow and relaxed martial art won't only improve your balance and develop your upper body strength and thigh muscles, it will also get your chi flowing gently, but surely and properly.

2. *Unblocking energies in the mind.*
   There is no better way to do this than through meditation.

What you need to do when unlocking mental chi is to turn the white noise in your head down. The brain is the most active organ in your body because you never really run out of things to think of -- even when sitting silently in the subway. You barely remember how or what happened, but you all of a sudden realize that you have been staring at the ground for 5 minutes. Whatever was inside, it consumed you instead of you consuming it. When you aim to allow the flow of chi in your mind, you need to practice mindfulness. It means you need to be aware of everything around you and everything that you are, and the first step to achieving this is by quieting the voices of your thoughts, and you can only achieve this through meditation.

Sitting down and training yourself to have a clear mind is difficult, especially if it's your first time doing it. You can start your training by taking your mind off of things initially. For example, when the memory of pending work on a weekend visits, avert your attention to something more productive, like gardening, knitting, cooking, or even cycling -- anything that can distract you from the memory. This will help your mind focus and you get to avoid getting lost in your thoughts.

3. *Unblocking energies in the heart.*
   Meditation has a huge role in this as well, but nothing beats acceptance and forgiveness in releasing emotions. This is actually the first step to attaining a positive outlook on life. By accepting the world's imperfections -- that to live will be difficult, that life will be unfair, and that it is in your very nature as a living and breathing being to suffer and feel pain -- handling every problem life throws at you won't affect you as it does now. And later on, you will understand that everyone on this lonely planet undergoes the same demise, even those covered in wealth and fame. So whenever someone wrongs you, finding

forgiveness in your heart won't be as difficult as it had been.

You won't be totally immune from despair, jealousy, hatred, anger and the likes, but it will be a lot easier for you to let these go and transform these to positive thoughts. Once your head clears, you will soon realize that the faults of others and what the universe has imposed on you are nothing but temporary events that can soon be forgotten.

As for memories that have left deep marks on your heart, understand that these will forever be a part of you. But know as well that drowning in self-pity, loathing, and despair will never bring you peace and positivity. Instead, think of how the event made you stronger, and identify the strengths you never knew you had. Realizing these things will not only raise your self-confidence, you will soon feel independent and whole.

Unblocking your energies is no walk in the park, and it may even take weeks to months, depending on how fast you can wholeheartedly implement the above habits and practices. Once you do, however, you will feel a change in your life. Everything will seem lighter, and at the same time, nothing will seem threatening. If you focus on your body hard enough, you may even begin feeling the flow of energy. May it be the steady movement of your heart and the stream of blood through your veins, or the actual flow of electric currents through your skin, it doesn't matter because they are all a part of your chi. What is important here is you feel it, and that it flows freely.

Understand, however, that this method of attaining the ability to heal using hands-on energy is not applicable for everyone. Perhaps it will boil down to your personality. Some people are more comfortable with discovering and improving things on their own. Furthermore, they give much intimacy to spiritual experiences, making them more adept in learning hands-on energy healing by themselves. If you are not this type, however, and assistance throughout the process will be beneficial, then you may opt to take formal reiki attunements where you will be guided and educated by a real reiki master.

Reiki Attunement

Aside from the type of energy that will flow through you, what makes reiki unique from other hands-on energy healing is *reiju*. This is the ceremony or initiation an incoming practitioner undergoes to formally begin his or her journey towards reiki. During this ceremony, a master will do the unlocking of chi for the student. Once the universal energy begins flowing, the trainee will undergo a course that typically consists of four levels, but are sometimes squeezed to three -- depending on the master's preferences. And during this course, they will experience a systematic process of attunement and empowerment to harness the ability to heal through reiki. Despite the minor differences between masters, the content of the training remains uniform since through the first students of Mikao Usui, and reiki courses always begin and end with the following:

Level 1: The First Degree

> Anyone can undergo the first degree, and as explained in the first chapter, even sceptics are welcome. This is where reiju falls, since the main concern here is opening the flow of energies on a physical level. After this initiation, students reportedly feel changes in their physiology. Some have felt the independent changing of temperature and vibration in their hands -- heating and cooling, and sometimes tingling. Despite being under the care of a master, however,

students are encouraged to practice reiki by themselves and on themselves, making meditation and self-reflection an important aspect of the first level.

Aside from this, students are also taught the history of reiki, proper hand placements, and participate in group practices. Understand that in this first level, different attunements will be undergone by the new practitioner. Normally, there are four attunements, but again, this will all depend on the master.

Level 2: The Second Degree

The only persons allowed to receive the second degree of attunement are those who have had sufficient training and knowledge from the first level, and it usually takes a minimum of 21 days to three months. There are masters, however, who combine attunements from the second degree with attunements from the first degree.

A higher level of energies need to be channelled in this level because the student will be taught how to heal at a distance. This means, they need to project their energy and not rely on light touches to deliver healing energies to the patient. Because of this, the focus of attunement and empowerment will be on the heart chakras. As explained earlier, the heart resonates the strongest and farthest magnetic field frequencies, hence there is no other way to accomplish and pass the second level without learning how to exert and control the hidden power of the heart.

Another lesson taught in this level is the use of symbols to amplify hands-on energy healing. Yes, reiki uses symbols to allow the practitioner to establish a deeper and stronger connection to universal energies. Depending on the symbol, the chi of the practitioner will be focused on what it represents. This may seem another incredulous claim of reiki, but this can actually be backed up by science.

Dr. James Oschman explained that the sight of symbols trigger electrical signals in the brain which can then alter the activity of frequencies of the person's magnetic fields. Mankind's most evolved sense is vision. Our eyes can detect and identify a multitude, if not all colors, and efficiently filter light to give us a better perception of the three dimensional world. Because of this, our brain dedicated a large and sophisticated portion of it to process information it receives from the eyes. The retina is connected to the nerves, and once it encounters specific visual events, it sends electrical impulses not only to the brain but to the rest of the body. In other words, looking at or visualizing an image trigger's certain neural activities in the brain which will then affect the body in certain ways. One good example of this is photosensitive epilepsy.

Level 3: The Third Degree

The third degree is where you learn to become a master, and achieving this level means the person is fully dedicated to reiki. Apart from the probability of taking years before attaining this level, one would have to explore several methods of practice and training, and this means not sticking to one master. A practitioner will have to add extra commitment to meditation to determine what road and which master should take them along the final stretch of their journey in reiki. Once they decide, however, they will receive the Master attunement and its corresponding symbol.

There happens to be an additional level of mastership in some courses of reiki, and the small difference lies between the person's ability to properly attune and guide those who seek to practice hands-on energy healing, and their ability to not. A practitioner can become a master but may not essentially feel comfortable in unblocking energies and training others. Of course, this requires an additional set of training and knowledge, and that's why some masters divide attunements to four levels.

A lot of other ceremonies, chants, and lessons are included in reiki courses that aren't discussed in this book. These are simply a bit too advanced and must be taught by a master because, as explained before, it must be experienced and sensed, and not merely memorized. Of course, you will have to remember the different chakra points of the body and the different symbols used in the healing process, but these will mostly rely on how well you control the energies in your body.

You may be weighing which option will better suit you -- to discover hands-on energy healing on your own, or to seek the guidance of a master. Understand, however, that both have its own advantages and disadvantages, and it's up to you to determine how both will affect your learning and training. Basically, if you plan to use reiki as a way to merely fight stress and fatigue, then opting for a masterless pursuit will be enough. But if you are interested gaining the ability to heal beyond this, then having your journey guided by a master is for you.

Chapter 4: A Quick Guide on Hand Placements for Specific Ailments

One does not simply touch the part of the body that aches to heal it. If you've been to a Chinese medicine shop, or any establishment that offers acupuncture, then you've seen those foot charts with points that, according to experts, are somehow connected to their labels, like 'liver', 'kidney', 'stomach', and such. The same goes for reiki, only that it carries a different chart.

To kickstart your hands-on energy healing as soon as possible, this book provides a quick guide on ailments and body parts for reiki self-treatments. You can practice with these when you feel you've managed to unblock your energies. If you're planning to work with a master, there's a huge chance you'll be given the same exercises in your first degree attunement, so it'll still benefit you if you learn these beforehand.

The body is divided to three major parts, and these are the head, body, and legs. In each part, different hand positions will be discussed, but understand that these only make up the tip of the iceberg.

Head

1. *Hands Over Eyes*
   Cup your hands over your eyes lightly. Keep your fingers closed and let your energies flow.

   This basically treats lymphatic diseases of all kinds. Aside from that, it is a good way to battle stress, burn outs, and colds, as well as hormonal imbalances. If you ever feel anything uncomfortable around your eyes, throat, sinus, face, ears, and nose, then this hand position will do the trick.

2. *Hands Over Temples and Crown*
   Place your palms over your temples, then fold your fingers over your crown. Allow the two middle fingers meet at the top of your head. Again, there's no need to add pressure on your touch.

   You will benefit more from this when easing any mental or emotional problems, as well as headaches and stress. Before walking in to exams, you can also do this for a couple of minutes to improve concentration. The body's immune and nervous systems will also be boosted, and like with the first hand position, it helps to fix hormonal imbalances.

3. *Hands at the Side of the Head*
   This time, lightly cup your hands over your ears, and allow the energies from your hands to flow.

   The ear is connected to a lot of other parts of the body in the acupuncture map, and basically, reiki affects and heals the same areas. But in general, it treats problems with your ears, throat, nose, and hearing. At the same time, it improves your balance and cures colds.

4. *Hands at the Back of the Head*
   Simply lay your palms at the back of your head, and position them as if you are holding a bowl. There's no need to add pressure, but if your hair is a bit puffy, then press your hands a bit.

   Whenever you feel something aching in your back, neck and brain, immediately assume this position. If you also have spinal nerve problems, whether you acquired it from an accident or from graceful aging, then practice this therapy for minutes to an hour a day, for several weeks up to months. This also makes a great way of drive away stress, worry, headaches, and colds.

Body

1. *Over the Throat*
   Envelope your neck with your hands. Meet the wrists in front of your throat then gently fold your fingers over the neck. Keep control of the weight of your hands because too much pressure will cause discomfort.

   This makes a good cure for communication difficulties or simple self-expression problems due to anxiety.

2. *Over the Shoulders*
   Simply place your hands over your shoulders. Make sure your collarbones and breast bones are covered.

   If you are having difficulty in accepting things, but you have no choice, then do this hand position and it will lessen your disdain over the matter. Also, if you have asthma, allergies, or any kind of lung problem, then make sure to practice this position.

3. *On the Breasts*
   Put your hands over the breast area.

   This basically clears matters of the heart, both emotional and circulation problems. Apart from that, this position helps your body improve the lungs, thymus, and immune system, and at the same time, fight asthma and allergies off.

4. *Under the Breasts*
   As the name states, place your hands over your ribs, in the area right under the breasts.

   If major digestive organs and problems are your concern then assume this hand position, because it helps and supports your spleen, pancreas and liver. Apart from that, your gallbladder, lungs, and sternum will also benefit from it. Emotions, worry, stress, nervousness and loss of control are the things you will be able to fight off with this position.

5. *By the Navel*
   Put your hands over the lower abdomen area, and let the tips of your fingers meet on your navel.

   Whenever you feel empty, depressed, or you simply cannot feel happiness, then assume this hand position. Just like with the previous one, major digestive organs and processes will be treated by this, along with the adrenal gland, kidneys, and gallbladder.

6. *Over the Hips*
   Feel for your pubic bones and place your hands over it, in an angle that follows the groin. Basically, your fingers should be pointing towards your genitalia.

   This hand position generally addresses sexual problems, may it be with your organs, or with your emotions. It also helps the body heal the kidneys, adrenal glands, and all other parts of the urinary system, and save you from tiredness and weight problems.

Back and Legs

1. *Above the Kidneys*

On your back, place your hands just around the waist area, above the kidneys. It's like you are in an akimbo, but your palms are flat on your back.

No one really knows what miracle moves around this position, but it happens to help you with relationship problems. In the physical aspect, this directly supports the lungs, heart, kidneys, diaphragm, lymph, and adrenal glands.

2. *Below the Waist*
   Hold the top area of your butt as if you have a backache. Your fingers should point towards your anus.

   This hand position also addresses problems with the reproductive and digestive system, as well as the pelvic area. When it comes to intangible things, expect your emotional and relationship problems to be soothed.

3. *On the Kneecaps*
   Wrap one hand over the knee cap, and place the other behind it. Treat one knee at a time.

   It's really far from the neck, but it does treat stiff necks, as well as headaches. If you are having problems with your lower body, whether knee injuries or energy blockages, then this hand position will do the trick.

4. *Around the Ankles*
   This doesn't have a correct hand position. As long as you are comfortable with it, and that your hands are wrapped around it, then that's good enough. Just make sure the back side of your ankle is also covered. As with the kneecaps, treat each separately.

The major areas this position affects are thyroid glands, lymph, neck, throat, and everything in the pelvic area. This can also clear energy blockages.

5. *Around the Foot*
   Place one hand on top of your foot, then put the other over your sole. Again, there's no need to worry about proper positions. Just be comfortable with it, and that's good.

   Going back to those acupuncture charts of the foot. According to experts, every part of the body is somehow connected to a certain point on the feet. This means that if you apply reiki healing on it, every part of the body will be treated. At the same time, it keeps you calm and grounded.

Keep in mind, however, that all of these are for self-treatments only. There are more positions involved when healing others, and the number of ailments it can cure are far more than the above enumerated. But as explained before, beginners should practice reiki on themselves first to try and feel for changes. Not only will this help you further clear energy blockages, it can also keep your mind, body, and heart healthy and ready to help others.

Conclusion

Thank you again for downloading this book!

I hope this book was able to help you learn more about Reiki healing!

The next step is to put these strategies into practice, and begin trying Reiki healing for yourself!

Finally, if you enjoyed this book, please take the time to share your thoughts and post a review on Amazon. It'd be greatly appreciated!

Thank you and good luck!

www.ingramcontent.com/pod-product-compliance
Lightning Source LLC
LaVergne TN
LVHW021743060526
838200LV00052B/3446